INFINITY

By Ana Thea

When I smiled and opened my eyes,

I saw infinity, you. Now the sky is

your infinity, and my smile is dusty.

Infinity

Introduction:
Welcome to the captivating world of "Infinity," a
collection that delves into the depths of love, drama, and
the human experience. Through a series of heartfelt
poems and thought-provoking quotes, this book invites
you to explore the complexities of relationships,
emotions, and the boundless nature of infinity itself.

Page 3:
As you turn to the third page of "Infinity," you embark on
a journey through the intricacies of love and the
profound impact it has on our lives. Here, you will
encounter a tapestry of emotions, where joy and pain
intertwine, and passion and heartache coexist.

Within these verses, you will find moments frozen in
time, capturing the essence of love's euphoria, its
tumultuous nature, and the longing that accompanies it.
Each poem is a window into the depths of the human
heart, vividly portraying the emotions that stir within us.

Amidst the pages, you will also discover poignant
quotes that resonate with the themes of love and drama.
These snippets of wisdom offer glimpses of truth and
introspection, inviting you to reflect on your own
experiences and perceptions of love's infinite power.

With "Infinity," you will find solace, inspiration, and a profound connection to the universal language of love. Whether you are seeking solace in times of heartache or yearning for the ecstasy of newfound love, these pages will accompany you on a journey of self-discovery and understanding.

So, turn the page, immerse yourself in the beauty of these verses, and let the words within "Infinity" touch your soul and ignite your imagination. Prepare to be captivated by the timeless drama of love and the infinite possibilities it holds.

Note: This is a fictional presentation of the first page of a book called "Infinity" containing love drama poems and quotes.

♡

I held onto an illusion, I believed,
A persistent truth within me.
It felt so real,
I could almost embrace the future.

Fragments of days fell upon my eyelids,
And I thought the sun shone brighter,
As it wept tears
For the unspoken words.

Yet, within these four walls,
I continue to conceal the same emotions,
Hoping that the fading dreams
Will forget them too.

I allowed myself to be carried away by thoughts,
And I now realise that the illusion is you,
While the reality resides within me.

4

♡ I allowed myself to be carried away like your thoughts, and I recognized
that "everything" is infinite. "Everything" except for you.
I let my thoughts fade into silence because they no longer breathe life into you . We are wandering souls, colliding haphazardly with reality, and we both forget to gaze at the same sky. We become lost in hollow words, and another day slips away. A day without yesterday. Each step counts the things we've forgotten. Have you forgotten?

I met you without searching for you,
and I fell in love without wanting to.
You are exactly what I asked of life,
something beautiful, and I believe you appeared.
In this life, I understood
after meeting you, that
as a person beside whom you could eat crumbs,
you can have a heart full.
That's how you remained the only battle
that I don't want to lose,
because in the noise that surrounds me,
you are my tranquillity.
You are the person who lifted me up
when I no longer believed in myself,
realising that you are
an angel, not a human.

Back then, I didn't understand
to look around me,
to appreciate what I had,
not knowing that nothing would be the same
since you went to heaven…

♡

You were the harbinger of spring,
Emerging from the depths of my soul,
Enclosed within the four walls
Of my fears...
I am the day that illuminated you,
The darkness in which you once immersed,
When hope seemed distant.

You were the whisper of the summer breeze,
Caressing me with dreams that arrived late,
I am the day when I crowned you the deity,
Ruling over heavens and earth,
Transcending the cardinal points.
You were the autumn's rainbow,
Adding hues to my smile,
Tinged with the dust of passing time.
I am the day when I embraced your thorns,
With tears that transformed,
Into a sea dried by the passage of time.

You were the warming sun,
During the winter I endured,
When the sky crumbled at my feet.
I am the day when I presented you a gift,
Though you may not remember.

You were... and you shall remain,
The sunset of seasons,
The past intertwined with my future.
You were... and I am the day when I left you behind.

You are as cold as ice,
but in your hands,
I melt immediately,
and everything that is good
in my soul,
is tied to you.
We give ourselves completely,
sacrificing everything,
without hope of reward:
is this what love means?!
In the end, meeting you
was my favourite coincidence,
and distance may keep two hands apart,
but not two souls!
And I chose to love you,
to love you as you are,
not as I wish you were,
because heaven is where you are.
In such a different world,
you are a miracle,
and if you could see my thoughts,
you would see only yourself,
discovering in the simplicity of a gesture,
the importance of a person.

And...ohh...what a beautiful dream!
We met by chance,
but we still wait for each other.

♡

A soul on one leg
Dizzy with melancholic thoughts
Sings its luck
With a thunderous voice.
There is a deathly silence
In my soul
The ephemeral birds fly
Reminding me of every flight
To think less than I feel.
Today is mine
Just like tomorrow
Everything wasn't yesterday
The same role played
The muse that animates me
Words reinterpreted
When the truth
Sleeps on the tongue
Everything is fine in a lie.

A kiss and a paperclip
Hanging from the braided tail
Playing with the sun's rays
What a shine!

A hand and a bracelet
Resting on the table
With a pencil and a notebook
They write about stories.

A smile and a colour
Invite thoughts to embrace
The soul that still lies
On the written pages.

Letters and wind petals,
Entangled in thoughts,
They turn into words
On the table of spring, courage.

Guitar and a linden tree
Hanging onto stories
Written with the left hand
Seasons.

♡

Pages of glasses
In a castle of metal
Shatter with blood
Out of helplessness.
I thought that if you were my infinity,
You would draw your infinity for me.
And yes, you did draw your infinity for me,
But not real, phantom-like.
Still a kind of infinity,
But not according to my expectations.
I couldn't understand you,
I couldn't accept you,
But I managed to move on from you,
By loving myself more.
And from the glass pages you offered,
I made flowers of ice.
Perhaps the fire within you
Will extinguish,
And you will see that the soul
Needs recognition,
Not falseness.

Your embrace is all I need, showing me that love comes
when I least expect it and is stronger than any other
feeling.

♡

A summer when the stars shone bright
Became my map
Where I look for you
To see you once again, at least.

It's a cold July summer
It's a month of memories
Of the scent of apricots
That was our umbrella
When we stopped running
After the rainbow.

From the horizon, the sun burns the field
Where we used to sleep
In each other's arms
And we both got intoxicated
With each other's scent.

The wind draws kites
From the gathered dust
And spreads melancholies
In the same place
Where we giggled
Creating the matrix of our dreams.

It's silent, a silent coldness
A breeze forgotten in time
Like my name next to yours.
It's something forever
That happened once upon a time, like never before.

I can recognize you even in the darkness by the way
you're silent and the way you breathe, and in your eyes,
I see the rest of my years beyond infinity.

♡

Lying has become our truth
And "nothing" defines our present...

I conceal unspoken words in the shadows,
Forgotten words and words unseen.
Darkness seeps into my soul,
Whispering to me about you,
How the sun is but a faded star
In my sky.

I hide my sharp thoughts,
Like icicles,
Don't remind me of the coldness
That lingers near you,
Ever since dreams perished.

I distance my heart from my soul,
It has frozen within its own tears.
Now is the time to grant it freedom,
For its emotions were the pillars of its joy,
A gift bestowed upon it by you.

I squint, searching for a smile,
Long lost and elusive,
Unsure of its whereabouts,
And whether it still exists.
I know it's not far from you,
But you remain distant from it.

♡

Scent of dreams,
Scattered upon a smile
Erased by illusions,
Try to believe
That nights are eternal.

Aromas that travel, create, chase... nostalgia;
Dusty in cities of white crystal
White as a lie.
Silence is forgotten
Within the silent scream of indifference.

Dreams lying in the swamp of night
Written on the edge of the image
Accidental events
From the hazy consciousness
An ego with a life.

Cold, eternal dream,
It continues to run on frosty paths
Echoing ephemeral tales
Until the early hours of the morning,
From the end of nocturnal thoughts.

♡

March, the month of forgetfulness,
They are waiting,
For the immeasurable longing.
From where I can't see
What you see...just see.
It's a warm March,
With the sound of a violin,
Guiding us on the hilltop.
You can hear it up until noon,
The love I have for you.
March colors,
Written, scribbled,
Adorn the plains,
Tossed in the wind.
You know, they transform into a song,
For you!
The young sun,
With its sunset to the east,
Rising in the night.
It caresses spring,
With our fairy tales.
It is the renewal of nature,
Of our souls,
And another year,
In which you are eternity,
And I, imagination.

♡When you love with longing, it never ends,
and everything becomes something beyond words.

I trust in vibes, not in words,
And I set myself free,
Let positivity be my shield.
My heart is like a child,
It doesn't understand endings,
Like a star, we all fall,
Until we reach the right place.
I am created from what was broken,
An ocean in a desert world,
My fire needs air to breathe.
I believe, perhaps the gaps in my life
Are part of the design,
Like some people stay with us
Even when they leave,
Like some people don't stay with us
Even when they are near.

♡I call you
With all my longing
Crazy angel
And I will wait for you after some time
Of weather
There's no more time.
In my heart,
From every drop of blood
The night blossoms
A core of a star.
If my grandmother were still alive
And she asked me if I still believe in monsters,
I would tell her about you;
The man who offered a kingdom
A kingdom where I cried,
Since I became a stone
Next to monsters who are not satisfied with a ray
They want a whole rainbow
Capturing dreams, leaving nightmares behind.
And even if we are forbidden
For each other,
In you, I found what I didn't find
What I didn't find in anyone else. Hell.
I don't know if you know, but
The only happiness is to have in your arms
The same person you have
In mind and soul.
I hope that one day,
We can forgive each other
Because we were not what we wanted
To be for each other.

♡ From the whole sky, I remain
With thunder and rain
To be my solace
When I lose my smile.
From all my thoughts,
I've left specks of glitter
Of rotten memories
To be imprinted there
Where I can't reach
When I feel love.
Among all the smiles,
I've built
Walls of glass with mirrors
And door without handles
From the outside, it smiles
Inside, the smile is drawn.

From everything I embrace,
Untold fantasies
Unspoken longing
Writing in the late morning sunset.

♡

I wrote to you in my mind,
Between the lines,
Lost innocence,
At the end of the embrace.

I gave you days,
A completely dusty mine.
Let me take everything of yours
From your abyss.

I brought you colors,
You chose gray.
You paint the sky black,
Paint the world in gray.

I looked at you at sunrise,
Searching for the sun.
I don't know you,
You are at sunset.

I carried you for days and years,
In the lost seasons.
I can feel you,
Unaware that you were never beside me.

And I write to you in vain,
At the end of the words,
Where you have departed,
The only crumbs of "you."

♡

So tell me, where should I go?
To the left, where nothing is right?
Or to the right, where nothing is left?

Meanwhile, tell them
I was the warmest place you knew
And that you made me cold.
Thank you for that
I may be as cold as ice,
But in the right hands, I'll melt.

You are the ghost of the sun in space
Between never and forever.
And maybe it's not about
Happy endings,
Maybe it's about the story
Where we write it with every indifference.

It's easy for me to be with you,
Hard to understand.
I'm an open book with
A language you don't comprehend.
There's another world inside me,
One you may never see...
It's not the future I fear
It's the repetition of the past that worries me.
It's not about change
I've heard your heart beating,
And you're in the dark
So I've decided to move on...

♡

It's half past nine
I'm ready to go
In search of you
With 666 boat of thoughts

It's not late
I'm lucky on fate
Ready to leave
Stepping out of the dream

Bon voyage to me
Embarking ships to see
Blue oceans and sand
With my favourite butterflies.

Hop on to get the fun
Thrills and soaking sun
Cool waters to dive
It's just half past ten

From hills to valleys
Ravines to open gullies
Riding through the bushes
It's more than half past eleven

Sleepy and tired
Off to bed, I quit
Hoping to wake up soon
Just before half past noon.

It's raining in the sky, on cheeks, in the night's fog
And crumbs of memories have smoked revived feelings.
I see life and everything, but... it's desolate...
She lives and yet is not alive
She can recognize happiness.
She is gentle, sensitive, wild
My love is full of hope.

About how it is to live with the soul in flames
Unspoken pains and moans in clenched fists
Endless searches and abrupt tomorrows
To be caressed by claws
A monster with a human face.

I seek the end of the night
To weave new memories
But today, yesterday, and tomorrow
The flames of the soul swim
And extinguish them with breaths taken from the
remaining crumbs.

I write to you in silent echoes.
Let me remember every time
How you are imagination
And I, I dream of the day.

I write to you,
On the edge of truth
Creating bridges
Towards the abyss.

I leave you on the footsteps of the wind
Travel there
Where falsehood calls you
For you have forgotten.

I remember you like yesterday
And today like never before
And I leave you with a memory
Letters written on eyelids.

Me...
You... do you exist?
A body of a ghost
That lives
In the forgotten silence
Of indifference.

♡

Sometimes it's a poem
Sometimes I write to your ego.
Sometimes it's just Saturday
Saturday on the first day,
Since I met you
Night with its mist
Silence screaming through the skin
Dreams gathered on stone clouds
Lost steps toward oblivion.
A Saturday from a story
Where the king is Rumplestiltskin,
Dragons are weapons
Who devour dreams,
Magic is a lie
weaving illusions,
And the rest are deadly flowers.
Saturday woven on lips
With cold fire that cools down
The nakedness of your words
What has become a stumbling stone
Of his Sunday imagination.

On that day, the gates of heaven closed,
And hell rose upon the earth
Bringing undying despair.
I embraced the thought that nothing
Can change the nights
The days filled with hope
And endless tears.
I kept telling myself that every payment,
I pay with the present
Surrounded by cold icicles
Frozen onto my soul
Scattered by longing.
It was cold and everything was frozen,
In broad daylight hidden in indifference
This was supposed to be my grave.
I gave myself entirely for love
At least as much as I know I am capable of
And I received poison that cured me of love.
Now it's empty and emptiness is silent
And the poison coursing through my veins
Gives me limitless freedom
To no longer know how it feels to love.

♡

If I had to choose between you and yesterday,
I would choose yesterday.
Yesterday was present in my life
But you... what or who are you?
If I were to offer a chance and a kiss,
I would give the kiss to you
And offer the chance to the present.
If I were to cry and embrace,
I would embrace you
And cry tears of joy to be able to forget you.
If I were to walk or run,
With you, I would go as far as I could
I would run to lose you behind.
If... you call me and write to me tomorrow,
I would make a story out of your words
And poetry for myself
To remember someday
That you are between being and not being
And I cling to your edge
Like a spider's web forgotten by time.

♡In your shadows, I constructed empires that crumbled with the first touch of a kiss.

♡

I thought I could lose
What I never had
Forgetting that rain remained on the earth
To remind me how it feels to love.
You are that he
That map
That abyss.
The sin I could never bear.
But if I hadn't driven you away,
You would have been the oxygen that filled me
My lungs with ashes
And the face that wouldn't make me smile.
You would have been mine.
Mine. Of a sick soul
Drowning in the bitterness of the past
But maybe you'll be in another life
Where I will be born worthy not to recognize you.
But sometimes I wonder
How does it feel to know that you destroyed a soul
That continued to be good
Even after you brought it down?
Do you know? Do you know what conscience is?

If I had to start over,
I would find you and love you,
But I don't promise to love you
More than I loved you in this life,
Because that would mean
I would never be born again

And I don't wish
To have never met you
Because you happened in the universe
But also in my own way
Leading me to the death of my soul
Where I had to learn
What I had become
Because of you: a phantom.

I believe I am a monster.
Only a monster
can make a pact
with another monster.

I bought lies,
with smiles and everything is fine
no one is happy.
Pain ignited me
in a war
continuing to go
through the mud
that is called something too.
While you thought you won,
I turned the mud
into ashes and the ashes
into stardust.
You may shatter dreams
But you can no longer break souls.
That's how I forgave you,
forgetting about you
detaching myself from your soul.
I don't know if I could forgive you
without pain
but if I didn't control my emotions
the emotions controlled me
in the failure of your arms.

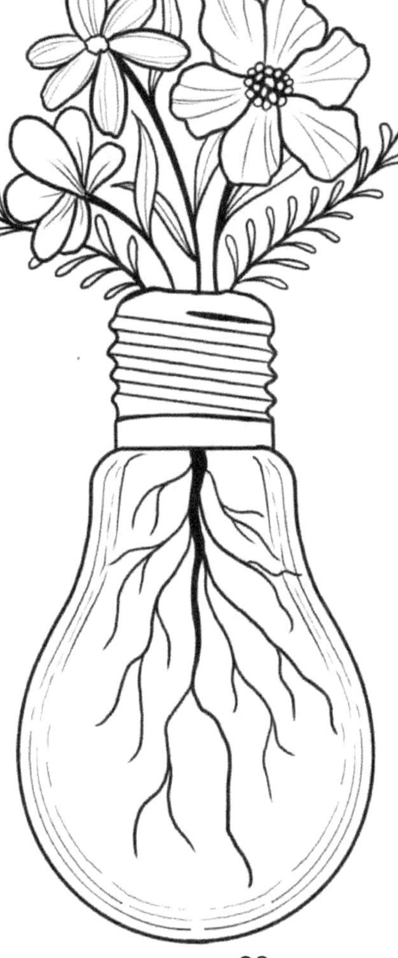

♡

I'm going to love the sound
of my feet walking away
from things not meant for me.

To new beginnings:
I can close this chapter
of my life and never look back
or I can flip through the pages,
revised old memories,
reflect on how different I once were.

That's the magic of
writing my own story--
.i'll meet new characters,
travel to new places,
face new obstacles
and the best part:
deciding how to overcome them
and then realising
I can.

♡Where there is no being to love, what does it mean to love without feeling?

I know my worth.
I paid a high price
For each time.
I write my feelings,
And let them live
The life you promised us.
I am like a castle,
From the outside, everything looks great,
Inside, it's in ruins,
Yet, I was open
For me to walk alongside you
On the same path.
I was stubborn and believed
That you could see life at least halfway
Through my eyes and half
Through your soul.
But I realised that, although I am
A castle in ruins, I have an entire kingdom,
And you... a whole sky.
And you promised me the sun,
Noise in the castle,
Painted drawings,
And the scent of dinner.
I opened my doors,
I was ready for everything for you,
I was ready to hear laughter,
Innocent steps singing through the castle,
And what is ours to become theirs,
To feel it throughout life,
Through your presence,

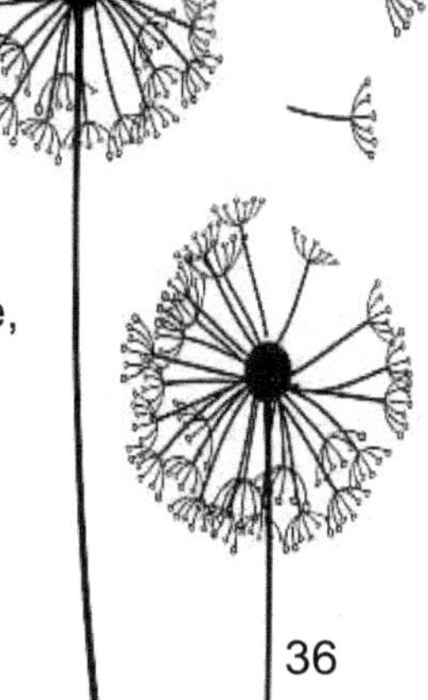

To fill our eyes with words
From clumsy things and ageing
Like time.
With doors open, I waited for you,
And I waited to see you step on the ground,
But you promised me in echoes,
And nothing is real. Only,
Time between us.
I still have to understand this,
We can meet
Through rain and wind,
Never on the ground,
Never in words, love, laughter.

Now you continue to promise me,
But the same echo,
Still the same, you know..

♡

I closed my doors,
And I can no longer trust you,
You are left to breathe illusions in vain,
We will both continue as usual, in,
Darkness.
Silence.
Raindrops.
Unfulfilled communication, forcibly torn.
Love unexpressed.
Yesterday.
Today.
Tomorrow.

♡

I am a piece of hell
Raised in purgatory
Running towards heaven
Believing I belong there.
I grew up staring at emptiness
Imagining boundless paradise
And how I would ever have
Happiness with an angelic smile.
I grew up with ideal dreams
Until I reached the dream of heaven.
My place was everything
Everything from the sky
From the sky, his infinite soul.
So much peace and love
Yet I couldn't find my peace
I kept hiding
The truth of what I am called.
And still, I was blind
In happiness, it couldn't make me happy.
When conditions diminished
I continued to be absent.
I was lost, didn't understand the purpose
And I went into hell.
I felt it for the first time
How thirsty the fire is
The truth, my hidden truth.
And then I realised that
Love is not enough for me
Love cannot open me up
And why I am.

Fire and darkness
It's my blood
And heaven, my mentor
Gave me wings to travel between purgatory and hell to feel my freedom
Without a soul.

♡

You will always be
my saddest goodbye.
And the most heartbreaking
story I will ever tell.
You will always be
the harder lesson I had
to learn
when I did not want to
end
the reason I learned
to never
put someone before me.
You will always be
the best thing that
never
happened to me.
Thank you for walking away.
If you hadn't let go of me,
I will not have
what I have
today.

I will not be
who I am
today.

♡
Yesterday I wakeup tired, extenuated
It hurt to open my eyes
And so I went back to sleep
And when I wakeup again
The sun was disappearing
And I lived in the darkness.

Today I wakeup sad
But I pushed myself to
Get up and get dressed
And it hurt at first
But then I smiled at the sun
And I walked in his rays.

Tomorrow I'll wake-up happy
And if not tomorrow
Then maybe next day
Or maybe it will take me
A week or a month
But I will get there.

♡You become the price you pay to obtain what you want.

♡ I needed a truth to know pain and a lie to know pleasure that made me who I am.

44

♡

"Be a free bird
And make your dreams a reality."

I flew so high,
So when I descended to the earth
Everything was different, unknown, and foreign.
I tried to understand
I tried to cry,
Believing that's how I bring to life
Souls, emotions, and love.
I resigned myself and rested
Where I thought life was.
When I woke up, it was just the grace of the cage
Which from the outside appears the brightest.
Inside, cold, cold like your soul.
A chill with its back to the sun
And closed eyes to make the lie seem real.
And the days passed into long nights
In silent echoes of loneliness
Indifference scorned by selfishness
Painting the bars of the cage.
Until I realised that the sun
Can only see me if
I start to fly again, as high as possible.
And I woke up realising that this freedom
Is paid with destiny.

♡

We always see the sky
less so the earth;
We are the chaff of dreams,
with trembling dreams
in poisoned echoes
of time and silence.
We seek the embrace of the soul,
to depart at sunset,
heading south
right from the edge of the world.
We remember yesterday and tomorrow,
without knowing
that today it is us
who are forgotten, remembered, and memorialised.
There, at the feet of the soul,
we leave a trace of "us"
written in an unknown
and everlasting love
that which we embrace forever.

♡One thing I'm sure of, our story didn't end in ashes, you continue to burn the light from the sky, and I search for it on the earth.

♡

When I embraced you,
I felt the infinite,
and I never thought
that nothing and no one could replace you
once you're gone.
But now I know why
you always told me
to stay strong and remain so;
Because you knew.
You knew that one day,
I would need the strength
to face your loss.
Even though I miss you more than I thought,
and I remember crying
more than I could bear,
feeling like the ground
was slipping beneath my feet,
time heals everything.
That's what I've been told.
But love sometimes comes at a cost.
And I pay.
Sometimes I smile. I know you're near.
But it's not enough. You're not here.
Years go by, and I'm not the same,
but in my heart, you'll remain.
You left with love
when you went to heaven,
and a part of me
remained with you.
Happy birthday!

♡At times, we may find ourselves departing from the people we hold dear, not out of selfishness, but driven by the weight of guilt. The remorse for having hurt someone we love can lead us down separate paths, as we grapple with the consequences of our actions.

♡

One day I received infinity
with its unknown,
and years of unique moments.
In the past days, I lost the ground beneath my feet,
yet the sky never stopped
to forget that feeling of "wow."
But if I could give one piece of advice,
it would be this: if we make mistakes,
never regret them.
What I am and what I have gained,
having everything, infinite, and hell,
felt beyond
where I never thought I would reach;
I found my mind victorious
when it was stronger
than my emotions.
The less I care,
the happier I am.
And I chose to be different;
I have the courage not to please everyone.

Do you know that linden tree
where spring used to smile at us
and time stood still
happy for us
that we shared the same thought
the same earth
isn't it the same destiny?!
Do you know that linden tree
from that summer
where we sought shelter
laughing in its shade
while we dreamed
of a foundation with a thread of hope
without knowing that the dreams
would disappear
with the first sunrise?!
Do you know that linden tree
where autumn drips
drops of rain
warm with love
in our souls
steaming with happiness
breathing in silence
which we didn't know
would soon come to an end?!
Do you know that linden tree
blessed by the winter queen
near our castle
lit with love and warm like
our immense souls

who didn't know
that if it snowed
it wouldn't reach the end
but only in solitude?!
Do you remember that linden tree?!
Those flowers...
That place...
That time?!
It's still here.
And you?

♡

In the truth of silence beyond the light,
shards of smiles are scattered,
beaten to nothingness
in the agony of memories
that forgot to forget
how it is to love and not hurt,
forgetting the last path
made of flowers of longing
to the greatest request
that is, asleep,
in the dusty crypt.
I find you every time,
every moment
allowed to flow,
alongside me for your yearning,
searching for that place,
that linden tree... the same feeling,
knowing that from there,
you know that time has not passed,
not even a moment;
time has remained frozen along with me.

♡Once, we were all united as a single entity. Now, we have become fragments of each other, sharing and embodying different aspects.

♡

There are days when...
I know that you have left,
and that time keeps passing
alongside the nostalgia of the present,
but there are days when...
even I forget
to fill my emptiness
with smiles and dreams,
and it remains for me to bring you to life.
Perhaps that way I save time,
and from there,
you sing to me like the last time,
with a warm smile
and your soul on the guitar.

There are also days when...
I hide my soul
and move forward,
with a lie on my lips,
"everything is fine."
I tend to believe that, yes,
the days pass by faster
when I don't miss you.
But there are also days
when I remember
that what we embraced
should never be let go,
and that I never let you leave.

Where do you place your breath
Before bedtime's gentle embrace?
In the depths of the soul,
Or within the realm of the mind's space?

And where does your ego reside,
In the realm of conscience's light?
Or does it find its dwelling place,
Within truth, yet polished with a lie?

Is it a question of where or never,
A choice between one way or another?
The answers lie within your heart,
Guided by wisdom and self-discovery.

♡There is a limit to how much one can forgive. You cannot continue to mourn the loss of futile hopes if oblivion has already overshadowed your dreams, knowing that they will never be realised. It becomes necessary to find a way to move forward and let go.

♡We embrace dreams when they transform into shining stars. Until that moment, we either breathe life into them or bury them deep within our souls, hidden from sight, believing that it is better to conceal them than to expose them and endure the pain they may bring.

♡If I moved on, I moved on with life, but I didn't leave you behind. You and I are still connected, rooted in the place where we began our journey together.

♡By being alongside the right person, one can experience spiritual and mental growth. Conversely, being with the wrong person can lead to becoming a mere legend, shaped solely by the circumstances of one's own destiny.

♡

If ever I could express
Who you truly are,
I would have just one word to say: absent.
If ever I were to depict the sun,
I would portray you, at times kind, at times excessive,
and at times not at all,
And most of the time, unreachable.
If ever I were to paint the day,
I would begin with the night, to capture the darkness
As beautiful as you, and paint the weary day
In colours drained like me,
Exhausted, still awaiting the embrace of darkness.
If I were to shed tears once more, I would remember
That I have nourished you enough with my tears,
Only to see your thorns grow.
But this time, I will cry with a smile,
To nurture my own life,
Which is finally as distant from you as can be.

♡

I would tell you something,
a message tethered to a kite,
describing the passage of time
since you departed from sight.

I would tell you something,
though frozen are the words,
yet memories don't fade away,
their essence forever preserved.

I would tell you something,
from here to where you reside,
let the clouds be our windows,
gazing upon each other with pride.

I would tell you something,
perhaps today or tomorrow,
each day drawing us nearer,
where we'll reunite, no sorrow.

♡The dandelion is our sun, which transformed into a puff of travelling stars, carrying you to heaven. And for me, the dandelion remains the sunrise, keeping alive the memory of how close we once were.

♡

As the night
Begins to descend
And the cool air
Caresses my skin
I gently close my eyes
And pretend
That you are here once again.

Your voice
Lingers in my mind
And your love
Softly envelops my heart
From this world
You may have departed
But our souls
Will never part.

♡The sky is brighter since you arrived there, and the silence that quivers with nostalgia has fallen onto the ground.

♡"Paint your own sky!" Do you remember?!
I painted the sky with colours and self-love until you
became a part of it.

♡

Forgotten moments, dusty,
They have hidden the words of the soul
And now I search for them
In the same place where they do not exist.

They exist! Not for me, not for you
Not for us, once upon a time
Maybe never
In another life.

♡
I carry a dream with you
towards twilight
where we used to stand
to gaze at our moment.

I believe, thinking,
until today, tomorrow, and if we will be once again
on the same cloud
where we were happy.
I love to remind you of the sun.

♡The ice crystals of truth melted into the lie and out came the gossip.

♡

I paint the sunrise with a feather
That fell from your hands
And the rain cools the fire
Giving birth to sparks
That melt the voices of thoughts.
It's enough for me and
I don't think about it anymore
That someone else could
Leave the same path
Without being marked
With the same mistakes
Without me believing
Still
That big dreams exist.
It's the same day
Every day and maybe
We're not here, but we remember
That we live through time and time
Come with us.

I have constantly sought hope
In the dawn of your world
Trying to find my gaze
Perhaps that's how I recognize
The guilt of being myself.
I have tirelessly written clichés,
Scratched stories,
Words trembling with emotion
Creating in you
A place where even you
No longer recognize yourself.

I consistently leave my mark
On the distance between us
And burn pages
To ignite for an ending
That came from the beginning.

♡I was stubborn for him. He was like a breath of fresh air, the sun on a cloudy day, and the missing puzzle piece in my life. He was everything I never knew I needed, and I was thrilled from the moment I met him.

But no matter how much I wanted to tell him how I felt, I couldn't find the right words. I was tongue-tied every time I was around him, and my palms would sweat at the mere thought of him. I had fallen hook, line, and sinker, completely under his spell.

I tried to play it cool, but it was like trying to catch a greased pig. He was always one step ahead, always out of reach. And even when I managed to get close, I felt like a fish out of water. I loved him to the moon and back, but I didn't know how to make him see it.

But then, one day, something clicked. Maybe it was the alignment of the stars, or maybe it was just sheer luck. But whatever it was, we finally locked eyes. It was like two peas in a pod, a match made in heaven, and love at first sight all rolled into one.

Now we're inseparable, like thieves without power, two peas in a pod, and joined at the hip. We're the perfect pair, the peanut butter to each other's jelly. We live happily ever after, and I wouldn't have it any other way.

The alarm goes off... What a dream! Hey, you! Up there in heaven, I think you guided my dream!

♡The colour that creates lies is called human being and the colour that creates truth is called character.

♡Difficult things twist the mind when we lose ourselves
within ourselves to our self.
Is it the same now?

You were my innocence
While I lost my colours
Trying to understand myself.
And yet, it's fortunate,
Now I don't even know who I am,
And you're left with the memory
Of how I once was.
Back then, I didn't have the courage
To tell you that you are
The soul that energises me,
But today I thank you.
You no longer know, I no longer recognize
The truth we used to believe in
In our attempt to build ourselves.
If we used to run away before,
It was because we believed,
Now we remain knowing what it is.
I don't know about you, but for me,
It's still an infinity,
But this time an empty infinity.

Remembered

You paint my dreams
With the sky and the rain
Unaware that you will be carried away by the wind
And I will always remember you;

Tell me it's just a dream
That nothing else exists
But I can't accept that
I will always remember us this way.

Time froze in that moment
With an uncertain future
Thousands of years in the same place
Holding onto the memories of you with courage.

One step closer to you
It becomes easier to carry on
With every breath I take
I love you for eternity.

♡If we love the devil, we accept the fires of hell.
If we love heaven, we accept to die daily.

♡Sometimes what we want is with us, but we look where it cannot be.

I painted the sky,
With rays of ash in my arms
Hoping that there
I will keep my dreams alive
Hanging from the stars of the night.
But the ash was scattered
Like us into nothingness.
You know, that nothing
When nothing was everything to us
Like now, when everything is nothing to us.

♡

Once upon a time, as never before.
I still remember how we started to talk.
I prayed with you, we trusted each other
Now... I still tell myself that I was never ready
To lose a universe, a dream, an eternity.
If I knew how it would be,
I made you take me
Into a world where promises are real.

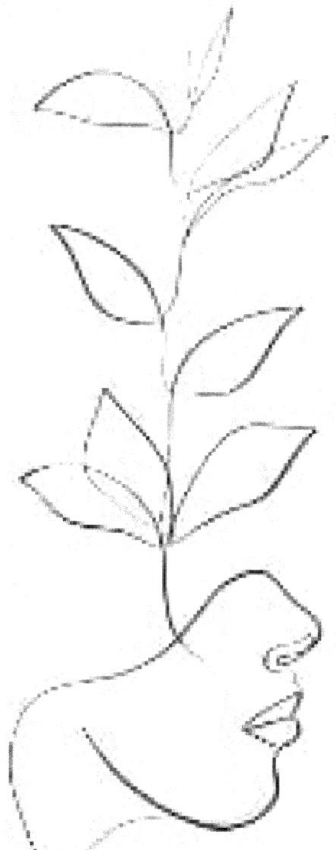

I cried so much, falling into the abyss crumbling
beneath my feet, that my heart told me to close
my eyes for a moment and let my soul heal me.

♡When I smiled and opened my eyes, I saw infinity, you.
Now the sky is your infinity, and my smile is dusty.

♡

You know, goodbyes
are not forever ...

The earth
never knew what
it was missing until
you came along.

And to soon
the sky grew envious
of the land
on which you walked.

And so heaven
opened its gates
and took you away
from me.

♡

Once you were,
Now you are a "no."
To yourself, you are a "yes."
You appear lost
In the aftermath,
And you beg for
Pieces of forgetfulness,
Thinking they will return
Until the present, which doesn't exist for us.
It is the ashes of history
Over the desert that surrounds us,
And your mind bows down
To ignorance.
And we continue...

♡It is written in the past, present, and future.
For me, it is written as heaven, breath, hope.

♡December is about you. The rest of the days are about us. What remains is... reality.
If the heart understands that the earth does not touch the sky... it wouldn't repeat that you are the one who went to heaven.

♡There are no words to carry them after your soul was frozen at the last breath of our 'everything'.

♡I am the embodiment of your imagination's awkwardness, providing solace to your soul when you hesitate to dream because you find yourself fully awake in my reality.

♡With certain individuals, it seems that you can only establish a superficial connection or a brief overview of who they are. However, with others, even an entire novel wouldn't be sufficient to capture the depth and complexity of their being.

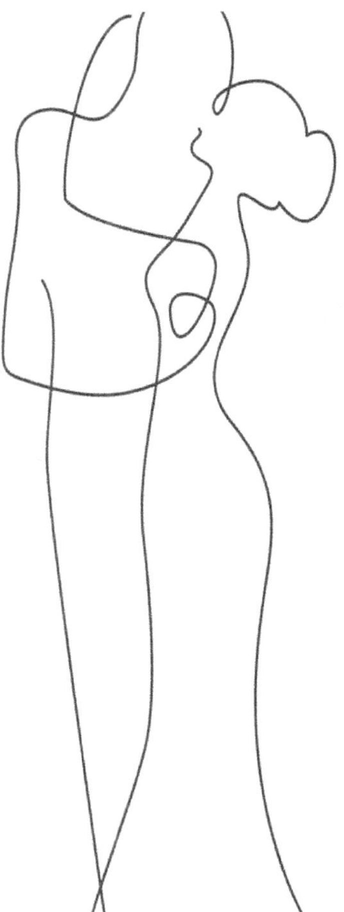

♡In a sky clouded with lies, it becomes difficult to paint dreamy stars.

♡From your "everything" I took a spark thinking it would give birth to fire. But... sometimes sparks only create storms that destroy everything in their path.

♡For you, it may be perceived as ego; for me, it's about setting standards. In life, we often encounter awakenings just in time, even as we stumble upon our own dreams, hoping that they will eventually come true.

♡With certain individuals, we embody aspects of ourselves that are otherwise unseen in the mirror.

♡I became a spectator of my own life, as my soul was departing from me, and I, blindfolded, believed that everything around me was real.

♡When I plucked roses, you questioned why I didn't reveal the pain caused by their thorns. All I can convey to you is that you, too, are a rose who remains indifferent to those who are pricked by your thorns.

♡If we were unaware of certain events that clandestinely weave tales in our minds, perhaps we would persist in a silence that veils our reality. Maybe we would traverse the days in dreams, until we arrive at the sunsets of weeks. Or, perhaps, amidst the uncertainty of "yes" and "no," we would find ourselves, together, here and there.

♡I love you, and I will continue to love you until the final day of my soul. Whether that day finds me here on earth or in heaven, I cannot know. However, I do believe that the soul possesses an infinite number of days.

♡I am difficult to the extent that you cannot understand due to your own pride.

♡In cages of desires, we confine the freedom that we sense, almost within reach but never truly ours.

♡
Under seasonal words,
I remember you dearly,
and I smile quietly,
knowing that you, from that place,
are still here with me.

♡I love you!!
"Until the end of time..."
I still love you...what is time?!

♡Sometimes it's better to know nothing, to remember nothing. Just to live.

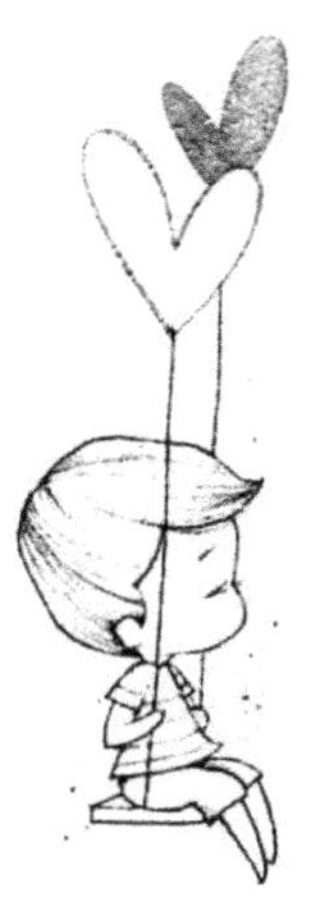

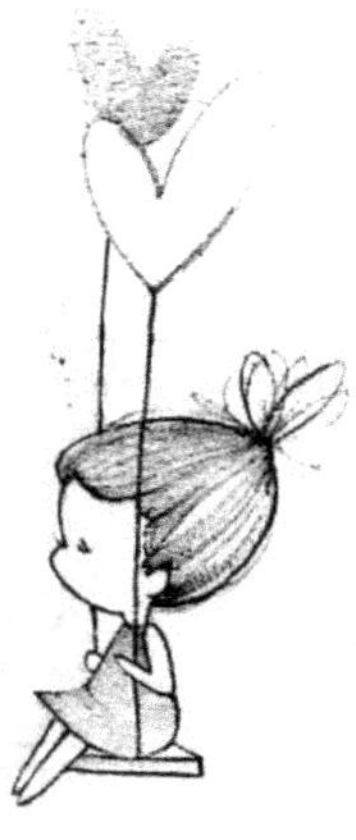

♡In my own better half, the rest are sparks, and the sky is where you are.

♡

I love your soul
empty, opaque, faded
or pure boundless
just like your words
when you're on the throne?

I love the best of "you all"
they read me a story
that changed me
to feel everything
in nothingness for
temporary happiness.

You're magical
like an illusion
just like my love
and we continue to live
in a world of stories
reality is for those who love.

♡Love is not just a feeling, it's a commitment to each other's happiness. It's facing the storms of life together, holding each other tight, and never letting go.

♡When love blooms, it's like you have found the missing piece of your puzzle, and suddenly everything falls into place.

106

♡You light up my life like fireworks in the sky.

♡If love had words, they would be written with the energy of the soul.

♡Pride gives birth to stories passed from ego to ego.

♡Cloudy, clear, colourful, like the sky is also longing.

♡It's morning... I wake up in everything I have. Family. Family is like a palette of colours. Each palette can create a simple drawing, a face of wax melted by time as well as an infinite universe of feelings.

The first non-color added to the palette was at the beginning of a rainy autumn. Meanwhile, like all non-colors, it will become colour. ,,The big black eyes touched his soul and his soul touched her heart.,, It was a non-color so innocent that you didn't think it could become a colour. The rain flowed non-stop... Somewhere at the end of the day it stopped. Those black eyes would embrace the first home.

The smell of rain impregnated in the earth and asphalt carried her towards the house.

♡Each star is waiting for us, lighting up the night.

♡Something that is past cannot return as past.

♡We kept asking ourselves why?! Why do we sometimes need sacrifices for survival? Although the years pass, I still do not manage to find the answer that fully satisfies me. What do you think? I remember in my childhood how I looked at everything as such and today with nostalgia. How our children look at things in a different context. The older we get, the less courage we have. In a huge ephemeral ocean, crossing all our memories of time.

Awoken by nostalgia, I look eagerly at everything that surrounds me. Our life is like a clock that has at the end the last hour. It's getting late... The moon is rising in the sky full of stars.

♡We are born from one soul belonging to one place.
The rest are journeys of a lifetime.

I painted the sky,
With rays of ash in my arms
Hoping from there
I will keep my dreams alive
Hanging from the stars of the night.
But the ash was scattered
Like us into nothingness.
You know, that nothing
When nothing was everything to us
Like now, when everything is nothing to us.

There are times when
It rains and rains
In which I am a nightmare
dressed in a daydream
from end to beginning
hanging strings of questions
which awaits its sunrise and
in the meantime on the azure blue sky I dance
with your grace around me.

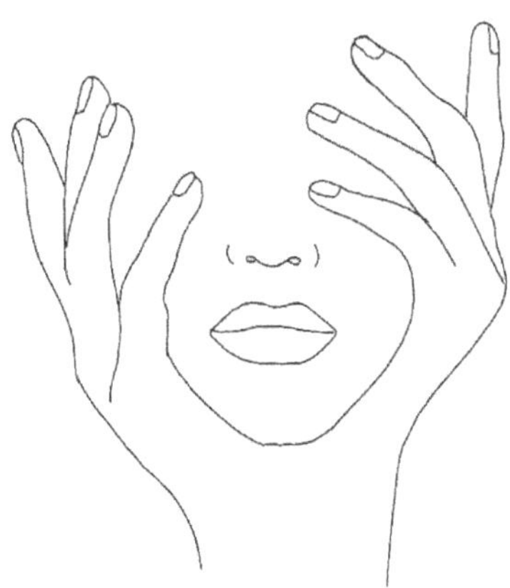

How many colours does spring wear?
It depends... Cold, wind, mud, rain...
Why not sunshine and birdsong?
Because we carry those ourselves.

How many colours are there in a poem?
Written by the broken heart of a winter?
A night of sighs, gone in search
Of smiles with the fragrance of springs.

How many colours can a flower have,
That blooms in the morning and sets in the evening?
Gusts of courage scattered on the horizon
By those who seek happiness in the world...

And how many colours do you see in me?
And in the words I write on paper?
One. Blue. It falls from the tears
Of the winter we hide within ourselves...

♡The most beautiful years are those years when you can embrace it all and let it go.

♡

When I left, I buried the past
As far away from the future as possible
And I carried with me my longing for you
Into a new life in the early days of autumn...

The clouds were crying before me
The days were passing, and I awaited winter.
Winter and its story with eternal smiles
I waited until the time of winter passed...

And I arrived on the first day of spring, realising,
That when I left, I didn't just bury the past
I also left behind winter and all the white stories
And I let autumn take the place of winter...

And once again, I cling to the stars
Perhaps they will remind you
To show me winter once more
Once more, without end...

Now it's spring... And you, the winter you once were,
You have ceased to appear in my world
Dreamer, the way you lived, the way you dreamed
You are now in your own world...

♡

I built myself a house with four walls
It had a floor, a roof, and three-quarters of a window
And I furnished it with shadows of emotions and material
trivialities.

I placed fear at the door as a guardian
And at the window, I sewed a curtain of
disappointments.
On the walls, I drew shattered worlds made of memories
And on the ceiling, I painted gates to my dreams.

The days flowed linearly, happily within the predictability
of events.
In the morning, I drank my tea alongside paper
sparrows, imagined from childhood
And during the day, I studied the theories of all possible
non-lives...

The years passed, and the house became so filled with
emptiness
That rarely did rays of light disturb the tranquillity of my
thoughts.

It was a late evening when I heard through the broken
window a deep sigh,
Deeper and sadder than the vastness of the night...
I didn't call upon fear for help, nor the paper birds,
I simply, timidly, set aside the disappointments and
through the bars of my soul

I caressed the loneliness that looked at me through the
window...
It had greying hair and shoulders burdened by the
weight of time.

And there, under the frozen shadow of my heart,
Together, until dawn, we wrote poems...
About life and flowers and love
And about God's most precious gift to us:
Spring!

Last night, as I slept, it rained with dreams
Dust of hopes and clouds,
Allowing the sun to dance
Throughout the night.

It was beautiful, peaceful
And my soul, too,
Like the aimless lakes
That hide magical lives.

Wildflowers with the scent of the sun,
And sparks of love
Showed me the trees
Embracing the celestial vault.

A single dream penetrated my soul
And grew in a joyful dance
On a bed of silver petals
Quiet like the dawn.

It became a dream in which it transformed
Into the most beautiful ray
And offered me tears
Of joy.

When evening came in my dream,
I spoke to the ray about the bright stars,
While fireflies wandered
Inquisitively through the gardens.

I tried to count them, but
The owl's song
Sang of awakening.
It's morning.

Dark morning,
With endless autumn rains
In a kingdom of ice
Without love...

When I met you,
It was a warm summer.
You were shining and transmitting good vibes to me
That's when I discovered that you are the sun...
Time passed, and the rainy autumn came.
I tried to search for your sun rays
But you were sitting on a throne, acclaimed by the world
And once again, I realised that the sun burns but heals
with love
And you are the king with two colours: white and black.
When winter sprinkled snowflakes, it was evening...
I saw you, and I saw my dreams gaining colour
But when morning came,
I understood that a king cannot please everyone
And you are not the night to bring colour to my dreams...

In the midst of spring,
I travelled with you through endless emotions
At the end of which, I discovered what
An amazing father you are...
And I understood that you have a soul
Courage, steadfastness, understanding, love
And I only have a frozen soul
On the edge of an abyss...

♡I grew up with the story of the dandelion. It was a tale passed down through generations, whispered in hushed tones as if it held some secret power. When the dandelion is in bloom, it looks at the sun and turns yellow, vibrant and full of life. But as time passes, it dries up, becoming pale like the moon. And then, in the night wind, its fluffy flower transforms into stars, scattering across the sky.

As a child, I was captivated by this story. I would spend hours in the fields, searching for dandelions, watching them sway in the breeze. I would imagine myself as one of them, yearning to be touched by the sun, to transform into something greater than myself.

But as the years passed, I forgot about the dandelion and its enchanting tale. Life took hold, and I became consumed by the mundane routines and responsibilities that come with growing up. I lost sight of the magic that once filled my heart.

It wasn't until I met someone that everything changed. They saw me as their dandelion, their soul. At first, I didn't understand what they meant. How could I be a dandelion? But as they spoke, their words resonated deep within me, awakening something long forgotten. They told me that I brought light into their life, just like the dandelion's vibrant yellow petals. They said that when I smiled, it was as if the sun itself was shining upon them. And when I laughed, it was like the gentle breeze carrying the dandelion's seeds.

I began to see myself through their eyes, and slowly, I started to believe in the power of the dandelion once again. I realised that I had the ability to bring joy and happiness to someone's life, just like the dandelion's transformation from flower to star.
But life has a way of teaching us lessons, and sometimes, it takes losing everything to truly understand the value of what we had. One day, the sun disappeared from my galaxy, leaving me in darkness. My world crumbled, and I felt as pale and lifeless as the dried-up dandelion.

In that darkness, I remembered the story of the dandelion. I remembered how it transformed into stars, even in the absence of the sun. And I realised that I, too, had the strength to shine, even in the darkest of times.

With each passing day, I began to rebuild my life, piece by piece. I embraced the pain and the loss, knowing that they were a part of my journey. And slowly, like the dandelion's transformation, I started to find my light again.
I became the dandelion, not just for someone else, but for myself. I bloomed, turning yellow with resilience and hope. And in the night wind, I let my dreams take flight, transforming into stars that illuminated my path.

I may not know what kind of dandelion I am, but I know that I am capable of bringing light and love into the world. The sun may be far away, but its warmth still resides within me. And the stars, those phantoms of my

lost dreams, remind me that even in the darkest of
nights, there is always a glimmer of hope.
So, I continue to grow, to bloom, and to shine. And as I
do, I carry the story of the dandelion with me, a reminder
of the power of transformation and the beauty that lies
within us all.

And today, like yesterday, it hurts...
To feel how your love burns
In flames of melted ice on glowing coals.

And today, like tomorrow, it is felt...
The same sensation that escapes tightly from the chest
That scratches every smile etched on the lips.

And today, like you...
It passes, smouldering, into the infinite void
Me here, and you just a step away from me, always
further ahead.

And... today... better not at all...
The same eyes with tears that burn on the cheek
And a heart shattered into countless pieces in your
colourless sky.

129

♡

It's raining in the sky, on the cheeks in the fog of the
night
And fragments of memories smoke, experiences
brought back to life.
I see life and everything, yet... it's desolate...
It lives and yet it's not alive
To be able to recognize happiness.
It's frail, sensitive, wild
My love entangled in hopes.

About what it's like to live with the soul in flames
Unspoken pains and riches clenched in fists
Endless searches and a harsh tomorrow
To be caressed by the claws
Of a monster in human form.

I search in the night for the end
To weave new memories
But today, yesterday, and tomorrow
The flames in my soul engulf them
And extinguish them with breaths taken from the crumbs
left behind.

If all the known and the unknown were known
Maybe today, maybe you, would have eyes towards the
sea
And I would have an oasis instead of a fire on the pyre
Maybe today, maybe with you I would merge my soul,
But today, yesterday, and tomorrow don't exist for us.
There isn't even an us...

♡The worst prison in the world is a home without peace:
just lies.

Once, you were the sun in the sky
Now, you are the sunrise of my soul.
We used to look at the same navy blue sky
Now you are the sky and I am the earth.
We are separated by a step and an eternity
Even if you're not so far away
Nothing seems darker than your absence.
You used to play the guitar with your endless smile
Now I write to God for you,
Knowing that one day we will meet again
In the same place of happiness
On the same day in December
At the same time, that's what has united us.
Now, for some, the present is a day for tomorrow
For me, the present is a day
When I will come to you soon.

Nothing managed to erase
That trace of a dream
Entangled in the corner
Of the eyes where tears
Have turned into crystals.

Nothing could take away
From the soul the burden
That lies dormant
Since I allowed myself to believe
That you wouldn't steal my reality.
Now madness or misfortune
Luck or fate
Scatter allusions
That shimmer in the wake of your steps.
Is it eternity or just a coincidence
Concocted by the fervour of having
Something from somewhere in my reality
Or is it a pleasant nightmare
And I have become addicted to it, to you.
To you, whom I never
Managed to find out who you are
Or why you're in my life.

♡I had a dream where I danced with your ghost.
In a grand hall with flickering chandeliers,
As champagne flutes were being carried around the
room and couples twirling in harmony.
It felt so real that when I woke up, I still heard the same
music playing.

♡In between heartbeats, in those tiny pauses where my soul breathes, that sacred space is where you are.

♡Fallen for you... like sunset's embrace,
Our love blooms, painting the sky with grace.
Colours ignite, a passionate display,
In your arms, I find solace every day.

With each passing moment, our spirits entwine,
In the twilight's glow, love's pure and divine.
Like the sun descending, casting golden light,
You are my beacon, my guiding star at night.

Together we dance, hand in hand we sway,
Lost in love's rhythm, the world fades away.
With you, my dear, my heart finds its tune,
Forever captivated, beneath love's moon.

Fallen for you... like sunset's embrace,
Our love, a masterpiece, time cannot erase.
In this eternal twilight, forever we'll be,
Bound by love's magic, forever you and me.

♡To awaken the conscience of humanity, it is never too late to confront the realities we once underestimated.

♡The soul runs through time like the seasons: it exists, it follows, it dies, it is reborn, and it forever remains.

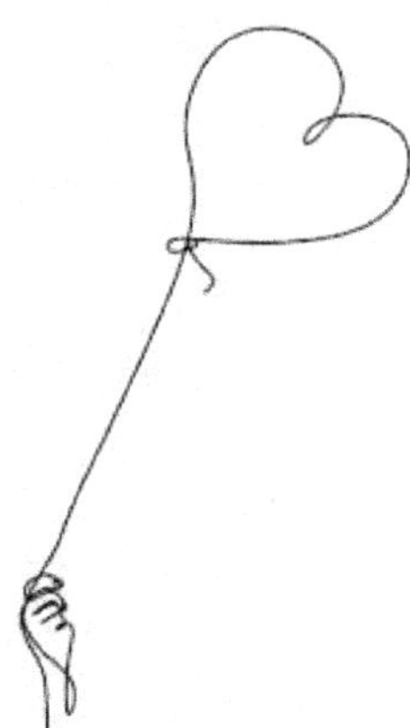

♡Maybe you are the one.
You and the three seconds of happiness when we wake
up in the morning.

♡You become the prize when you pay the price for what
you truly desire.

In love's domain, a truth unfurled,
"You become the prize," the world's pearls.
For when you pay the price, my dear,
To claim the love that you revere.
In whispers of longing, hearts ignite,
Guided by passion, burning bright.
You journey forth, undeterred and bold,
Seeking the treasure worth its gold.
Through trials faced, and sacrifices made,
Love's worth emerges, no price too great.
With every step, you forge your way,
To win the prize, where hearts will sway.
In this dance of souls, a destiny weaves,
Where love's sweet magic softly breathes.
For in your pursuit, you'll come to see,
The cherished prize you were meant to be.
So fear no cost, let love be your guide,
As you become the prize, side by side.
For in the depths of love's embrace,
You find your worth, your sacred place.

In the depths of my being, a flame does reside,
A devotion unyielding, by your side.
Till the final breath of my soul's embrace,
An eternal bond, woven in time and space.
Through life's winding journey, hand in hand we tread,
A love unspoken, yet felt and spread.
With every heartbeat, a symphony of desire,
Igniting our spirits, setting them afire.

Across earthly plains or celestial heights,
Our souls entwined, bound by love's light.
For the soul knows no bounds, no limit or end,
Infinite days, a tapestry to transcend.
With each passing moment, our souls align,
A symphony of emotions, divine and refined.
No words can capture this love's grand art,
But in every breath, I pledge my heart.

So whether on earth's stage or in heavens above,
Our souls entwined, a testament to love.
Till the last day of my soul's vibrant flame,
Together we'll dance, in eternal acclaim.

♡

In the sky clouded with lies,
a sombre hue,
Where truth is obscured,
 dreams hidden from view.
Amidst the haze,
 the stars elude your sight,
Their ethereal glow veiled
by deceit's might.
Yet fear not, dear soul,
for hope still remains,
For within your heart,
resilience sustains.
Though the canvas may be
tainted and unclear,
Your spirit perseveres,
 undeterred by fear.
With each brushstroke,
you paint a different scene,
Embracing truth and breaking free from the routine.
No longer bound by the clouds' deceptive guise,
Your dreams take flight,
reaching infinite skies.
For in the realm of honesty and grace,
New constellations form,
 filling empty space.
Where once there were lies,
now stars brightly gleam,
Illuminating your path,
like a cherished dream.
So let not the clouds of deceit hold you tight,

Unveil the truth and let your spirit ignite.
In the sky of possibilities,
 let your art unfurl,
And paint a celestial world,
a dreamscape, pure.
For in the sky clouded with lies, you'll find,
That honesty and dreams can intertwine.
With each stroke of truth,
as your colours blend,
A masterpiece emerges,
transcending the end.

144

♡

In the realm of forgiveness, there's a limit to bear,
Endlessly forgiving, burdens too heavy to share.
No longer can you kiss the grave of vain hopes,
When oblivion has settled, dreams tangled in ropes.
For some dreams, alas, are destined to fade,
Lost in the realms of what could have been made.
When the veil of truth reveals their fateful end,
It's time to let go, to heal and transcend.

Like a bird in flight, your spirit can soar,
Breaking free from the chains of dreams of yore.
Though the pain may linger, acceptance takes hold,
Releasing illusions, embracing truths bold.
Let go of the ghosts that haunt your past,
Embrace the present, where your happiness can last.
For in letting go, you find strength anew,
To forge a path where dreams can come true.

So bid farewell to the dreams that can't be,
Embrace the beauty of what's meant to be free.
With a heart unburdened, find solace and peace,
As new hopes and dreams begin to release.
For in the depths of your spirit's embrace,
Lies the power to move on, to find your own grace.
Though dreams may perish, new ones can bloom,
From the ashes of the past, a future will loom.

♡If I had the power to bring something to life,
I would choose to revive the ashes that have
been scattered by the wind, even when
the wind itself no longer blows against destiny.

♡At times, we can find ourselves lost in the passage
of time, spending years in pursuit of
comprehending the complexities of life.

♡We enter the world in a state of uncertainty, and throughout our lives, we have the agency to choose whether to reside in a state of suffering (hell) or in a state of bliss (heaven). However, as we journey through adulthood, we often find ourselves collecting fragments of our true selves, leading us back to a path of self-reflection and growth (purgatory).

♡To possess and to be aware, rather than lacking and remaining ignorant, is the essence of truth within the lie.

♡Culture is the leap of habits to adapt from one day to
another.

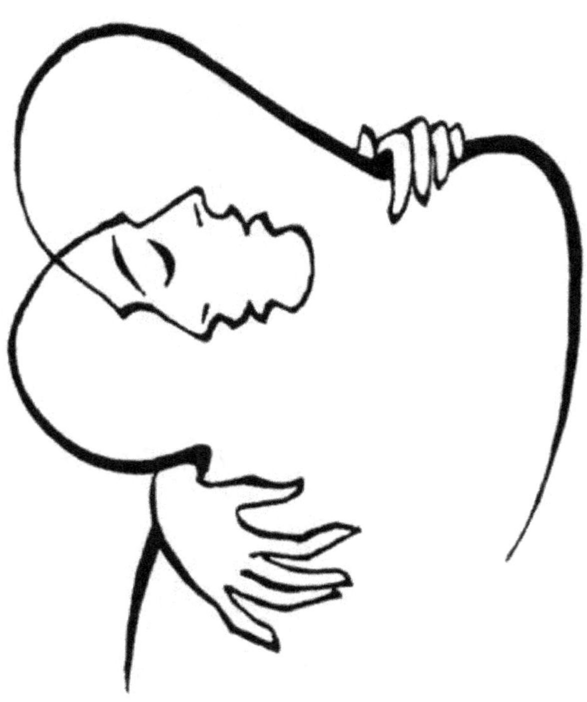

♡If you take drops from the ocean with you, can you transform them into blue seas or rivers of fire?

♡But if we wait for tomorrow, does yesterday catch up with us, and today ceases to exist?

♡Being a parent is a unique experience that can neither be categorised as solely hard nor easy. It encompasses a range of challenges, joys, and responsibilities. Raising a child requires carrying a significant part of their well-being, growth, and development with us as parents. It involves nurturing, guiding, and supporting them throughout their journey.

♡From the vast sky, you are the sunrise that pours
nostalgia, painting the present moment on the earth.

♡Maybe time has passed, but I can still smell your perfume.

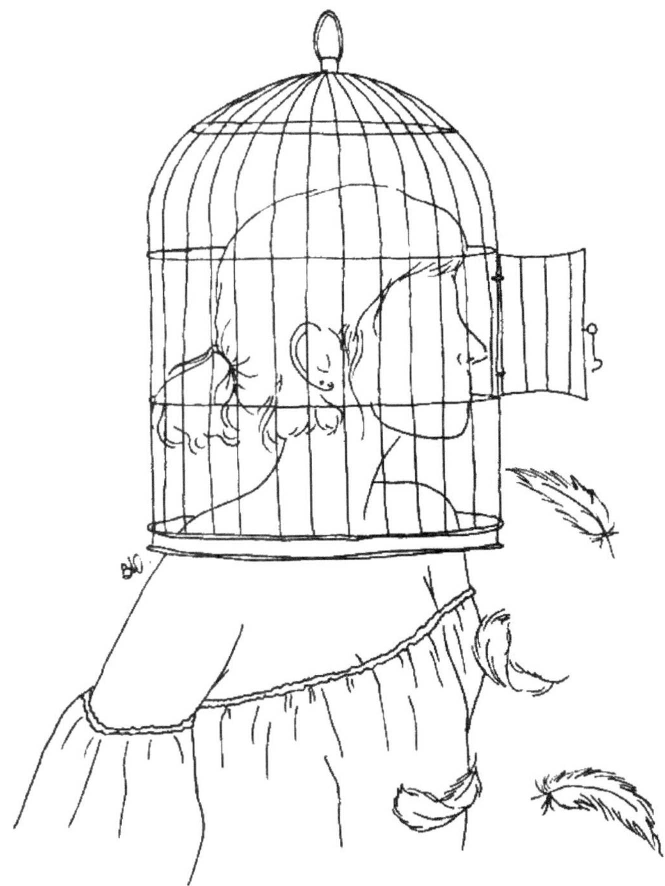

♡There are no words that can describe the description of a word that has no word to show the depth of the soul.

♡Sometimes even everything is not enough for you when you no longer recognize your soul in the mirror.

♡When you lose everything, you start to create everything.

♡I have never limited my imagination. She lives with me breathing your memory.

♡I never knew that love could be so beautiful and yet so painful. But in the end, it's worth all the tears and heartache because loving you is the greatest adventure of my life.

♡True love is a flame that never fades, a force that cannot be tamed, and a journey that requires both courage and vulnerability.

♡We can write unrealistic dreams and still fulfil them.

162

♡Today is the day we wrote immortal stories.

♡I write with longing to remind you that the sky is the same here, and it is expected for you to tread upon the earth again.

♡You wrote the sealed verse that delights my soul.

♡In the mind without feeling there is no truth.

♡On untrodden roads are seeds of dreams carried by
the wind where they await their birth.

♡Love is a drama where hearts become actors,
emotions take centre stage, and the plot twists
are both exhilarating and heartbreaking.

♡Time took you but forgot to take your memory too.

169

♡Before you, I was me.

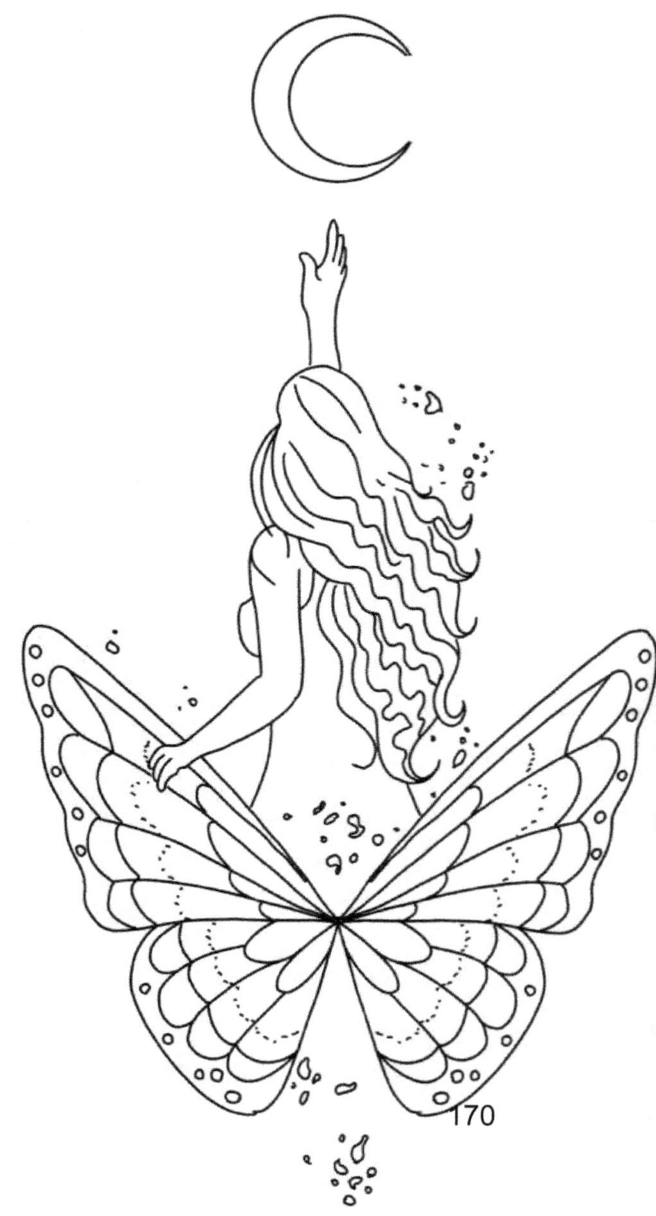

♡Love, like a journey into the unknown, embraces the enigma of happiness, revealing treasures awaiting those brave enough to explore.

♡In the dark is the warmest hug and in the light, the
most treacherous smile. With each one, we build our
peace or despair.

♡Half of the people lie with their lips;
The other half with their tears.

173

♡Next to the right person you develop spiritually and mentally. Next to the wrong person you become a legend of your own destiny.

♡In life, we either live or continue.

♡I told you that I will look for you where you will be, but you are the one who finds me every time.

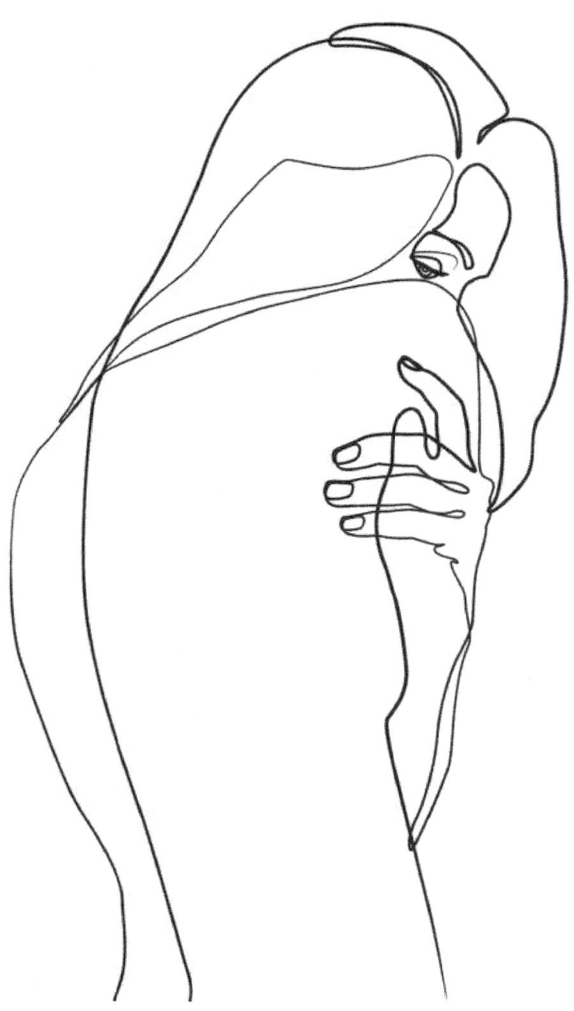

♡There will be men who fall in love with your skin and others who drown themselves in everything that lies beneath. This is how you know, this is how I know.